CHECKERBOARD BIOGRAPHY LIBRARY

U.S. PRESIDENTS

The
United States Presidents

HARRY S. TRUMAN

ABDO Publishing Company

Heidi M.D. Elston

visit us at
www.abdopublishing.com

Published by ABDO Publishing Company, 8000 West 78th Street, Edina, Minnesota 55439.
Copyright © 2009 by Abdo Consulting Group, Inc. International copyrights reserved in all
countries. No part of this book may be reproduced in any form without written permission from the
publisher. The Checkerboard Library™ is a trademark and logo of ABDO Publishing Company.

Printed in the United States of America, North Mankato, Minnesota.
012009 042013

Cover Photo: Getty Images
Interior Photos: Alamy pp. 8, 29; AP Images pp. 14, 25; Corbis p. 16; Getty Images pp. 5, 13, 18,
    27, 28; Copyright Unknown, Courtesy of Harry S. Truman Library p. 15;
    Courtesy of Harry S. Truman Library pp. 9, 11, 17, 23; Library of Congress p. 19;
    National Archives p. 21; National Park Service p. 10; U.S. Air Force p. 20

Editor: Megan M. Gunderson
Art Direction & Cover Design: Neil Klinepier
Interior Design: Jaime Martens

Library of Congress Cataloging-in-Publication Data

Elston, Heidi M. D., 1979-
  Harry S. Truman / Heidi Elston.
    p. cm. -- (The United States presidents)
  Includes index.
  ISBN 978-1-60453-476-4
  1. Truman, Harry S., 1884-1972--Juvenile literature. 2. Presidents--United States--Biography--
Juvenile literature. I. Title.

  E814.E59 2009
  973.918092--dc22
  [B]
                                2008040273

CONTENTS

HARRY S. TRUMAN

Harry S. Truman was the thirty-third president of the United States. He rose to this position after President Franklin D. Roosevelt died. Truman had served as Roosevelt's vice president for just 83 days.

As a young man, Truman was a farmer. He then served in the Missouri **National Guard** during **World War I**. After failing in business ventures, he turned to politics. Truman was an honest politician. He soon gained a national reputation.

In 1944, President Roosevelt decided to run for a fourth term. Truman campaigned as his **running mate**. He and Roosevelt won the election. The next year, Roosevelt died suddenly. Vice President Truman then became president.

As president, Truman made some of the hardest decisions in world history. The nation was spending billions of dollars to fight **World War II**. And, the United States had recently developed an **atomic bomb**. Truman worked hard to lead his country through this critical time.

TIMELINE

1884 - On May 8, Harry S. Truman was born in Lamar, Missouri.

1919 - Truman married Elizabeth "Bess" Wallace on June 28.

1922 - Truman was elected a Jackson County judge.

1926 - Truman was elected presiding judge of the Jackson County Court.

1934 - Truman won election to the U.S. Senate.

1941 - The United States entered World War II; the U.S. Senate established the Truman Committee to investigate defense spending.

1945 - On January 20, Truman became vice president under Franklin D. Roosevelt; President Roosevelt died on April 12, and Truman became president; on August 6, the United States dropped an atomic bomb over Hiroshima, Japan; the United States dropped an atomic bomb on Nagasaki, Japan, on August 9; World War II ended.

1947 - Truman proposed the Truman Doctrine; Congress passed the Twenty-second Amendment; Congress passed the Taft-Hartley Act; on July 18, Truman signed the Presidential Succession Act.

1948 - On November 2, Truman was elected president; on April 3, Truman signed the Marshall Plan into law.

1949 - Truman was inaugurated for his second term on January 20; the United States joined 11 countries in forming the North Atlantic Treaty Organization.

1957 - The Harry S. Truman Library opened in Independence, Missouri.

1972 - On December 26, Harry S. Truman died.

DID YOU KNOW?

Harry S. Truman's middle initial does not stand for anything. His parents could not decide on a middle name. It was between *Shippe*, in honor of his father's father, and *Solomon*, for his mother's father. So, Truman's parents agreed on *S* to honor both grandfathers.

Truman read every book in the public library in Independence, Missouri, by age 14.

Truman was the first president to travel underwater in a submarine.

Truman was the first president to give a speech on television.

While Truman was president, Jackie Robinson became the first African-American man to play modern Major League Baseball. Robinson joined the Brooklyn Dodgers in 1947.

MISSOURI BEGINNINGS

Harry S. Truman was born on May 8, 1884, in Lamar, Missouri. He was the son of Martha Young Truman and cattle trader John Anderson Truman. Harry had a brother named John Vivian and a sister named Mary Jane.

FAST FACTS

BORN - May 8, 1884

WIFE - Elizabeth "Bess" Wallace (1885–1982)

CHILDREN - 1

POLITICAL PARTY - Democrat

AGE AT INAUGURATION - 60

YEARS SERVED - 1945–1953

VICE PRESIDENT - Alben Barkley

DIED - December 26, 1972, age 88

John and Martha Truman

In 1890, the Truman family moved to Independence, Missouri. There, Harry attended school. When he was nine, Harry had to start wearing glasses. This kept him from playing sports.

Harry also caught **diphtheria** that year. He was sick for many weeks and had to quit school. When he got better, Harry attended summer school to catch up. He later claimed he skipped third grade because he had studied so hard!

Harry liked to play the piano and read. His favorite author was Mark Twain. Harry spent much of his spare time at the public library in Independence. He read many novels, history books, and encyclopedias. Harry even read the entire Bible twice before he was 12.

Harry's grandparents lived on a farm in Grandview, Missouri. During the summer, Harry and his brother and sister visited them. The children rode horses, swam, and helped with the farmwork.

The Truman family farm in Grandview

In high school, history was Harry's best subject. Mathilda Brown was his history teacher. She said, "I doubt if there was a student in any high school in the country who knew more of the history of the United States than Harry did."

In 1901, Harry graduated from high school. He then applied to the U.S. Military Academy at West Point in New York. However, he was not accepted because of his poor eyesight.

Harry then moved to Kansas City, Missouri, to look for work. There, he worked at a drugstore and the *Kansas City Star* newspaper. He was also employed by a railroad company and a bank.

After five years, Harry moved to Grandview to help run the family farm. He worked there for the next ten years. During this time, Harry tried some different business ideas. He invested in a mineral mine and an oil company. Both times, he lost his money.

In 1917, the United States entered **World War I**. At the time, Harry was still a farmer. He was also a member of the Missouri **National Guard**. So in 1918, he went to France as an **artillery** captain. Harry fought well in several battles. He returned home in 1919.

In France, Harry and his men saw action in the Saint Mihiel and Meuse-Argonne offensives.

TURNING TO POLITICS

On June 28, 1919, Truman married Elizabeth "Bess" Wallace. They had been childhood sweethearts. The Trumans had their only child on February 17, 1924. They named her Mary Margaret.

Meanwhile, Truman tried his luck at business again. In 1920, he invested in a men's clothing business in Kansas City. It made money for two years before failing in 1922.

Truman then turned to politics. A powerful politician named Tom Pendergast helped him get started. With Pendergast's support, Truman was elected a Jackson County judge in 1922. At that time, Truman entered the Kansas City Law School. For two years, he took night classes. He felt this would help his political career.

Truman ran for reelection in 1924 but lost. "I was broke and out of a job with a family to support," he said. "But, I had a lot of friends and pulled through until 1926."

In 1926, Truman was elected **presiding judge** of the Jackson County Court. He oversaw many county expenses. Truman did his job well. He became known as an honest politician.

The Truman family

SENATOR TRUMAN

In 1934, Truman decided to run for the U.S. Senate. With Pendergast's support, Truman won the election. He took office in January 1935. Senator Truman worked hard and was honest. He soon gained people's respect. He won reelection in 1940.

Campaigning for the U.S. Senate in 1934

The following year, the United States entered **World War II**. Truman was concerned about government money being spent on the war. He wanted to make sure this money was not wasted.

Truman asked the Senate to create the Committee Investigating the

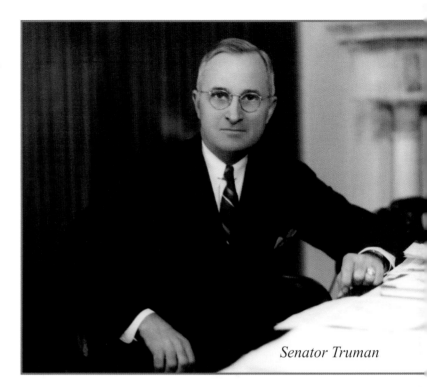

Senator Truman

National Defense Program. This group is commonly called the Truman Committee. It was designed to stop wasteful spending.

The Truman Committee helped save the U.S. government about $15 billion. Now, Truman was one of America's best-known politicians.

THE 1944 ELECTION

In 1944, the **Democrats** chose President Franklin D. Roosevelt to run for a fourth term. But, they were worried about his health. If Roosevelt died, his vice president would become president. So, he needed a strong **running mate**.

The Democratic Party was split. For many Democrats, current vice president Henry A. Wallace's views were too extreme. Former U.S. **Supreme Court justice** James Byrnes was a popular choice. However, many felt he was too **conservative**. Supreme Court justice William Douglas was another favorite.

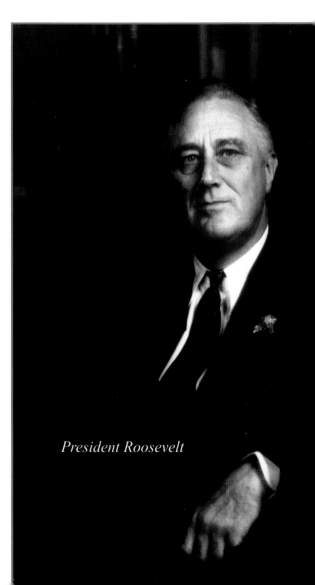

President Roosevelt

Truman was also a possible candidate. The Truman Committee investigations had earned him a national reputation. But he was happy in the Senate. Yet President Roosevelt pressured him anyway. Finally, Truman accepted the nomination.

Roosevelt's **Republican** opponent was New York governor Thomas Dewey. Dewey's **running mate** was Ohio governor John Bricker.

Roosevelt and Truman easily won the election. Roosevelt was **inaugurated** on January 20, 1945. That day, Truman became his vice president. As vice president, Truman made no important decisions. Roosevelt rarely met with him or asked for his advice.

A memo from Truman regarding the vice presidential nomination

WORLD WAR II ENDS

On April 12, 1945, Vice President Truman was called to the White House. There, he learned that President Roosevelt had died suddenly. By law, Truman would become the next president.

Truman took the oath of office at 7:09 PM. Now, he faced a big challenge. He was not prepared to be president. Yet many aides helped Truman, and he learned quickly.

Two weeks after taking office, Truman learned of a top-secret program. It was called the Manhattan Project. The U.S. government was making an **atomic bomb**.

Meanwhile, the **Allies** were winning **World War II** in Europe. On May 7, 1945, Germany surrendered. With this, the war in Europe ended. But in Asia, America was still at war with Japan. Many people were dying every day.

Truman now faced one of the hardest decisions in world history. He had to decide whether to use the atomic bomb against Japan. Just one bomb could destroy a city.

Manhattan Project members tested a plutonium bomb on July 16, 1945. It was exactly like the bomb used on Nagasaki, which was nicknamed "Fat Man."

18

U.S. Supreme Court chief justice Harland F. Stone administered Truman's 1945 oath of office.

Truman warned Japan about the bomb. He said America would use it if Japan did not stop fighting. Truman hoped this threat would force Japan to surrender. But Japan refused.

On August 6, 1945, the United States dropped an **atomic bomb** over Hiroshima, Japan. Two-thirds of the city was destroyed. Three days later, another bomb destroyed the city of Nagasaki. Japan finally surrendered. Truman's tough decision took thousands of Japanese lives. Yet **World War II** was finally over.

After the war, world leaders helped form the **United Nations (UN)**. Member countries agreed to work for world peace. Truman

A mushroom cloud rose above Nagasaki following the drop of an atomic bomb.

approved of the **UN**. In December 1945, the Senate and the House voted to join.

Truman's problems in Europe were not over. Shortly after **World War II** ended, the **Cold War** began. World War II had left many countries ruined. Those countries had no money to rebuild. Now, the Soviet Union was steadily gaining control of nations in Eastern Europe.

Truman feared the Soviet Union would also take control of Greece and Turkey. He knew America needed to provide aid. So in March 1947, he proposed the Truman Doctrine. This plan gave Greece and Turkey money to rebuild.

In June, U.S. **secretary of state** George Marshall proposed providing money to rebuild all of Europe. This action is called the Marshall Plan. However, the Soviet Union would not allow Eastern European nations to receive aid. So, the plan covered only Western European nations. President Truman signed the plan into law April 3, 1948.

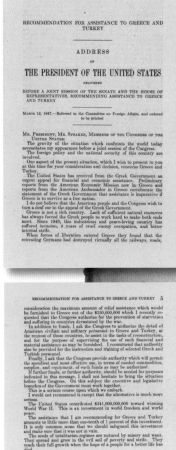

Truman Doctrine

DOMESTIC AFFAIRS

President Truman also faced problems in America. By January 1946, more than 1 million U.S. workers were on strike. They refused to work until they were paid more money.

By June, home prices were rising. And the cost of goods such as food, clothing, and automobiles was greatly increasing. Voters blamed Truman and his fellow **Democrats**. As a result, the **Republicans** won a majority in Congress in the November elections.

In 1947, Congress passed the Twenty-second **Amendment** to the U.S. **Constitution**. Any future president could serve only two terms or a total of ten years. The amendment did not go into effect until 1951.

Also in 1947, Congress passed the Taft-Hartley Act over Truman's **veto**. This placed limitations on labor unions. On July 18, President Truman signed the Presidential Succession Act. This altered the order of succession to the office of the U.S. president.

PRESIDENT TRUMAN'S CABINET

SECOND TERM
JANUARY 20, 1949– JANUARY 20, 1953

- **STATE** – Dean Acheson
- **TREASURY** – John W. Snyder
- **DEFENSE** – James V. Forrestal
  Louis A. Johnson (from March 28, 1949)
  George C. Marshall (from September 21, 1950)
  Robert A. Lovett (from September 17, 1951)
- **ATTORNEY GENERAL** – Tom C. Clark
  J. Howard McGrath (from August 24, 1949)
- **INTERIOR** – Julius A. Krug
  Oscar L. Chapman (from January 19, 1950)
- **AGRICULTURE** – Charles F. Brannan
- **COMMERCE** – Charles Sawyer
- **LABOR** – Maurice J. Tobin

FIRST TERM
APRIL 12, 1945– JANUARY 20, 1949

- **STATE** – Edward R. Stettinius
  James F. Byrnes (from July 3, 1945)
  George C. Marshall (from January 21, 1947)
- **TREASURY** – Henry Morgenthau Jr.
  Frederick Moore (from July 23, 1945)
  John W. Snyder (from June 25, 1946)
- **WAR** – Henry Lewis Stimson
  Robert P. Patterson (from September 27, 1945)
  Kenneth C. Royall (from July 25, 1947)
- **DEFENSE** – James V. Forrestal
  (from September 17, 1947)
- **NAVY** – James V. Forrestal
- **ATTORNEY GENERAL** – Francis Biddle
  Tom C. Clark (from July 1, 1945)
- **INTERIOR** – Harold L. Ickes
  Julius A. Krug (from March 18, 1946)
- **AGRICULTURE** – Claude R. Wickard
  Clinton P. Anderson (from June 30, 1945)
  Charles F. Brannan (from June 2, 1948)
- **COMMERCE** – Henry A. Wallace
  W. Averell Harriman (from January 28, 1947)
  Charles Sawyer (from May 6, 1948)
- **LABOR** – Frances Perkins
  Lewis B. Schwellenbach (from July 1, 1945)

President Truman kept a sign on his desk that read, "The Buck Stops Here." This common phrase means responsibility is not passed beyond this point.

POLITICAL UPSET

The year 1948 brought another election. The **Democrats** wanted to nominate General Dwight D. Eisenhower for president. However, Eisenhower refused. So, the party chose Truman instead. Senator Alben Barkley of Kentucky was his **running mate**.

Once again, the **Republicans** nominated Thomas Dewey for president. His running mate was California governor Earl Warren.

Southern Democrats who opposed the **civil rights** program of their party formed the Dixiecrat Party. They chose South Carolina governor Strom Thurmond to run for president. Mississippi governor Fielding Wright was his running mate.

Many Americans thought Dewey would win the election. But Truman campaigned hard. He traveled across the nation and gave more than 300 speeches.

The election took place November 2. Before the final results were in, radio reports declared that Truman had lost. The front page of the *Chicago Daily Tribune* read, "Dewey Defeats Truman."

Truman received less than half the popular vote. Still, he won the election.

But, Truman won the election with 303 electoral votes! Dewey received 189 electoral votes, and Thurmond earned 39. It was one of the biggest political upsets in U.S. history. The **Democrats** also won control of Congress.

FOREIGN AFFAIRS

On January 20, 1949, Truman was **inaugurated** for his second term. Soon after, the United States and 11 other nations formed the North Atlantic Treaty Organization. This group works to keep peace among its members. It also protects them from common enemies. At the time, this included the Communist Soviet Union.

In August 1949, the Soviet Union tested an **atomic bomb**. Truman worried the Soviet Union would become more powerful than America. So, he decided the United States should make more atomic weapons. The arms race had begun.

The Korean War started on June 25, 1950. North Korea was a Communist country. It wanted to take over South Korea. Truman worried about the spread of Communism. He sent U.S. soldiers to help **UN** forces defend South Korea. U.S. general Douglas MacArthur commanded the UN forces in Korea.

Chinese Communists had joined North

SUPREME COURT APPOINTMENTS

HAROLD H. BURTON - 1945
FRED M. VINSON - 1946
TOM C. CLARK - 1949
SHERMAN MINTON - 1949

More than 50,000 American soldiers died during the Korean War.

Korea in the fighting. So, MacArthur wanted to launch an attack on China. But, Truman wanted to keep the fighting in North Korea. MacArthur publicly criticized Truman. So in April 1951, Truman removed MacArthur from his command. The war ended in 1953.

TRUMAN GOES HOME

From 1948 to 1952, the White House was under construction. So, President Truman and his family had to live in Blair House. It was across the street from the White House.

On November 1, 1950, Truman survived an **assassination** attempt at Blair House. After the incident he said, "A president has to expect those things." He conducted his usual business that day.

In 1952, Truman decided not to run for reelection. He retired to his home in Independence, Missouri, the following year. There, Truman enjoyed a quiet life with his wife.

Truman's friends raised funds to build the Harry S. Truman Library in Independence. It opened in 1957. On December 26, 1972, Harry S. Truman died. He is buried in the courtyard of the library.

Truman was an honest, hardworking man. He became president at one of the most troubled times in U.S. history. Today, Harry S. Truman is best remembered for his leadership at the end of **World War II**.

In retirement, Truman remained active in politics.

The Truman Home in Independence, Missouri, is a national historic site. The house was known as the "Summer White House" during Truman's presidency.

OFFICE OF THE PRESIDENT

BRANCHES OF GOVERNMENT

The U.S. government is divided into three branches. They are the executive, legislative, and judicial branches. This division is called a separation of powers. Each branch has some power over the others. This is called a system of checks and balances.

EXECUTIVE BRANCH

The executive branch enforces laws. It is made up of the president, the vice president, and the president's cabinet. The president represents the United States around the world. He or she oversees relations with other countries and signs treaties. The president signs bills into law and appoints officials and federal judges. He or she also leads the military and manages government workers.

LEGISLATIVE BRANCH

The legislative branch makes laws, maintains the military, and regulates trade. It also has the power to declare war. This branch consists of the Senate and the House of Representatives. Together, these two houses make up Congress. Each state has two senators. A state's population determines the number of representatives it has.

JUDICIAL BRANCH

The judicial branch interprets laws. It consists of district courts, courts of appeals, and the Supreme Court. District courts try cases. If a person disagrees with a trial's outcome, he or she may appeal. If the courts of appeals support the ruling, a person may appeal to the Supreme Court. The Supreme Court also makes sure that laws follow the U.S. Constitution.

QUALIFICATIONS FOR OFFICE

To be president, a person must meet three requirements. A candidate must be at least 35 years old and a natural-born U.S. citizen. He or she must also have lived in the United States for at least 14 years.

ELECTORAL COLLEGE

The U.S. presidential election is an indirect election. Voters from each state choose electors to represent them in the Electoral College. The number of electors from each state is based on population. Each elector has one electoral vote. Electors are pledged to cast their vote for the candidate who receives the highest number of popular votes in their state. A candidate must receive the majority of Electoral College votes to win.

TERM OF OFFICE

Each president may be elected to two four-year terms. Sometimes, a president may only be elected once. This happens if he or she served more than two years of the previous president's term.

The presidential election is held on the Tuesday after the first Monday in November. The president is sworn in on January 20 of the following year. At that time, he or she takes the oath of office:

I do solemnly swear (or affirm) that I will faithfully execute the office of President of the United States, and will to the best of my ability, preserve, protect and defend the Constitution of the United States.

Line of Succession

The Presidential Succession Act of 1947 defines who becomes president if the president cannot serve. The vice president is first in the line of succession. Next are the Speaker of the House and the President Pro Tempore of the Senate. If none of these individuals is able to serve, the office falls to the president's cabinet members. They would take office in the order in which each department was created:

Secretary of State

Secretary of the Treasury

Secretary of Defense

Attorney General

Secretary of the Interior

Secretary of Agriculture

Secretary of Commerce

Secretary of Labor

Secretary of Health and Human Services

Secretary of Housing and Urban Development

Secretary of Transportation

Secretary of Energy

Secretary of Education

Secretary of Veterans Affairs

Secretary of Homeland Security

BENEFITS

- While in office, the president receives a salary of $400,000 each year. He or she lives in the White House and has 24-hour Secret Service protection.

- The president may travel on a Boeing 747 jet called Air Force One. The airplane can accommodate 70 passengers. It has kitchens, a dining room, sleeping areas, and a conference room. It also has fully equipped offices with the latest communications systems. Air Force One can fly halfway around the world before needing to refuel. It can even refuel in flight!

- If the president wishes to travel by car, he or she uses Cadillac One. Cadillac One is a Cadillac Deville. It has been modified with heavy armor and communications systems. The president takes Cadillac One along when visiting other countries if secure transportation will be needed.

- The president also travels on a helicopter called Marine One. Like the presidential car, Marine One accompanies the president when traveling abroad if necessary.

- Sometimes, the president needs to get away and relax with family and friends. Camp David is the official presidential retreat. It is located in the cool, wooded mountains in Maryland. The U.S. Navy maintains the retreat, and the U.S. Marine Corps keeps it secure. The camp offers swimming, tennis, golf, and hiking.

- When the president leaves office, he or she receives Secret Service protection for ten more years. He or she also receives a yearly pension of $191,300 and funding for office space, supplies, and staff.

PRESIDENTS AND THEIR TERMS

PRESIDENT	PARTY	TOOK OFFICE	LEFT OFFICE	TERMS SERVED	VICE PRESIDENT
George Washington	None	April 30, 1789	March 4, 1797	Two	John Adams
John Adams	Federalist	March 4, 1797	March 4, 1801	One	Thomas Jefferson
Thomas Jefferson	Democratic-Republican	March 4, 1801	March 4, 1809	Two	Aaron Burr, George Clinton
James Madison	Democratic-Republican	March 4, 1809	March 4, 1817	Two	George Clinton, Elbridge Gerry
James Monroe	Democratic-Republican	March 4, 1817	March 4, 1825	Two	Daniel D. Tompkins
John Quincy Adams	Democratic-Republican	March 4, 1825	March 4, 1829	One	John C. Calhoun
Andrew Jackson	Democrat	March 4, 1829	March 4, 1837	Two	John C. Calhoun, Martin Van Buren
Martin Van Buren	Democrat	March 4, 1837	March 4, 1841	One	Richard M. Johnson
William H. Harrison	Whig	March 4, 1841	April 4, 1841	Died During First Term	John Tyler
John Tyler	Whig	April 6, 1841	March 4, 1845	Completed Harrison's Term	Office Vacant
James K. Polk	Democrat	March 4, 1845	March 4, 1849	One	George M. Dallas
Zachary Taylor	Whig	March 5, 1849	July 9, 1850	Died During First Term	Millard Fillmore

PRESIDENT	PARTY	TOOK OFFICE	LEFT OFFICE	TERMS SERVED	VICE PRESIDENT
Millard Fillmore	Whig	July 10, 1850	March 4, 1853	Completed Taylor's Term	Office Vacant
Franklin Pierce	Democrat	March 4, 1853	March 4, 1857	One	William R.D. King
James Buchanan	Democrat	March 4, 1857	March 4, 1861	One	John C. Breckinridge
Abraham Lincoln	Republican	March 4, 1861	April 15, 1865	Served One Term, Died During Second Term	Hannibal Hamlin, Andrew Johnson
Andrew Johnson	Democrat	April 15, 1865	March 4, 1869	Completed Lincoln's Second Term	Office Vacant
Ulysses S. Grant	Republican	March 4, 1869	March 4, 1877	Two	Schuyler Colfax, Henry Wilson
Rutherford B. Hayes	Republican	March 3, 1877	March 4, 1881	One	William A. Wheeler
James A. Garfield	Republican	March 4, 1881	September 19, 1881	Died During First Term	Chester Arthur
Chester Arthur	Republican	September 20, 1881	March 4, 1885	Completed Garfield's Term	Office Vacant
Grover Cleveland	Democrat	March 4, 1885	March 4, 1889	One	Thomas A. Hendricks
Benjamin Harrison	Republican	March 4, 1889	March 4, 1893	One	Levi P. Morton
Grover Cleveland	Democrat	March 4, 1893	March 4, 1897	One	Adlai E. Stevenson
William McKinley	Republican	March 4, 1897	September 14, 1901	Served One Term, Died During Second Term	Garret A. Hobart, Theodore Roosevelt

PRESIDENT	PARTY	TOOK OFFICE	LEFT OFFICE	TERMS SERVED	VICE PRESIDENT
Theodore Roosevelt	Republican	September 14, 1901	March 4, 1909	Completed McKinley's Second Term, Served One Term	Office Vacant, Charles Fairbanks
William Taft	Republican	March 4, 1909	March 4, 1913	One	James S. Sherman
Woodrow Wilson	Democrat	March 4, 1913	March 4, 1921	Two	Thomas R. Marshall
Warren G. Harding	Republican	March 4, 1921	August 2, 1923	Died During First Term	Calvin Coolidge
Calvin Coolidge	Republican	August 3, 1923	March 4, 1929	Completed Harding's Term, Served One Term	Office Vacant, Charles Dawes
Herbert Hoover	Republican	March 4, 1929	March 4, 1933	One	Charles Curtis
Franklin D. Roosevelt	Democrat	March 4, 1933	April 12, 1945	Served Three Terms, Died During Fourth Term	John Nance Garner, Henry A. Wallace, Harry S. Truman
Harry S. Truman	Democrat	April 12, 1945	January 20, 1953	Completed Roosevelt's Fourth Term, Served One Term	Office Vacant, Alben Barkley
Dwight D. Eisenhower	Republican	January 20, 1953	January 20, 1961	Two	Richard Nixon
John F. Kennedy	Democrat	January 20, 1961	November 22, 1963	Died During First Term	Lyndon B. Johnson
Lyndon B. Johnson	Democrat	November 22, 1963	January 20, 1969	Completed Kennedy's Term, Served One Term	Office Vacant, Hubert H. Humphrey
Richard Nixon	Republican	January 20, 1969	August 9, 1974	Completed First Term, Resigned During Second Term	Spiro T. Agnew, Gerald Ford

PRESIDENTS 26–37, 1901–1974

PRESIDENT	PARTY	TOOK OFFICE	LEFT OFFICE	TERMS SERVED	VICE PRESIDENT
Gerald Ford	Republican	August 9, 1974	January 20, 1977	Completed Nixon's Second Term	Nelson A. Rockefeller
Jimmy Carter	Democrat	January 20, 1977	January 20, 1981	One	Walter Mondale
Ronald Reagan	Republican	January 20, 1981	January 20, 1989	Two	George H.W. Bush
George H.W. Bush	Republican	January 20, 1989	January 20, 1993	One	Dan Quayle
Bill Clinton	Democrat	January 20, 1993	January 20, 2001	Two	Al Gore
George W. Bush	Republican	January 20, 2001	January 20, 2009	Two	Dick Cheney
Barack Obama	Democrat	January 20, 2009			Joe Biden

"Every segment of our population and every individual has a right to expect from our government a fair deal." Harry S. Truman

WRITE TO THE PRESIDENT

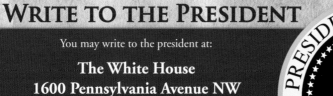

You may write to the president at:

**The White House
1600 Pennsylvania Avenue NW
Washington, DC 20500**

You may e-mail the president at:
comments@whitehouse.gov

GLOSSARY

allies - people, groups, or nations united for some special purpose. During World War II Great Britain, France, the United States, and the Soviet Union were called the Allies.

amendment - a change to a country's constitution.

artillery - the branch of an army that uses and manages weapons that discharge missiles.

assassination - the act of murdering a very important person, usually for political reasons.

atomic bomb - a bomb that uses the energy of atoms. It is thousands of times more powerful than a regular bomb.

civil rights - the individual rights of a citizen, such as the right to vote or freedom of speech.

Cold War - a period of tension and hostility between the United States and its allies and the Soviet Union and its allies after World War II.

conservative - of or relating to a political philosophy based on tradition and preferring gradual development to abrupt change.

Constitution - the laws that govern the United States.

Democrat - a member of the Democratic political party. Democrats believe in social change and strong government.

diphtheria (dihp-THIHR-ee-uh) - a disease that affects the throat and can cause death.

inaugurate (ih-NAW-gyuh-rayt) - to swear into a political office.

justice - a judge on the U.S. Supreme Court.

National Guard - one of the voluntary military organizations of the U.S. Army and Air Force. Each state, each territory, and the District of Columbia has its own National Guard. Each unit is commanded by individual state governors and the president.

presiding judge - the judge that manages the county courts and their
   schedules. He or she also appoints judges to specialized courts and oversees
   meetings of the judges.

Republican - a member of the Republican political party. Republicans are
   conservative and believe in small government.

running mate - a candidate running for a lower-rank position on an election
   ticket, especially the candidate for vice president.

secretary of state - a member of the president's cabinet who handles relations
   with other countries.

Supreme Court - the highest, most powerful court in the United States.

United Nations (UN) - a group of nations formed in 1945. Its goals are
   peace, human rights, security, and social and economic development.

veto - the right of one member of a decision-making group to stop an action
   by the group. In the U.S. government, the president can veto bills passed
   by Congress. But Congress can override the president's veto if two-thirds
   of its members vote to do so.

World War I - from 1914 to 1918, fought in Europe. Great Britain, France,
   Russia, the United States, and their allies were on one side. Germany,
   Austria-Hungary, and their allies were on the other side.

World War II - from 1939 to 1945, fought in Europe, Asia, and Africa. Great
   Britain, France, the United States, the Soviet Union, and their allies were
   on one side. Germany, Italy, Japan, and their allies were on the other side.

WEB SITES

To learn more about Harry S. Truman, visit ABDO Publishing Company on
the World Wide Web at **www.abdopublishing.com**. Web sites about Harry
S. Truman are featured on our Book Links page. These links are routinely
monitored and updated to provide the most current information available.

INDEX